THRILL SEEKERS
DIVING WITH SHARKS

BY RYAN NAGELHOUT

Gareth Stevens
Publishing

Please visit our website, www.garethstevens.com. For a free color catalog of all our high-quality books, call toll free 1-800-542-2595 or fax 1-877-542-2596.

Library of Congress Cataloging-in-Publication Data

Nagelhout, Ryan.
Diving with sharks / by Ryan Nagelhout.
  p. cm. — (Thrill seekers)
Includes index.
ISBN 978-1-4824-3286-2 (pbk.)
ISBN 978-1-4824-3287-9 (6-pack)
ISBN 978-1-4339-9900-0 (library binding)
1. Sharks — Juvenile literature. 2. Scuba diving — Juvenile literature. I. Nagelhout, Ryan. II. Title.
QL638.9 N34 2014
597.31—dc23

First Edition

Published in 2014 by
Gareth Stevens Publishing
111 East 14th Street, Suite 349
New York, NY 10003

Copyright © 2014 Gareth Stevens Publishing

Designer: Michael J. Flynn
Editor: Therese Shea

Photo credits: Cover, p. 1 Stephen Frink/Photographer's Choice RF/Getty Images; p. 5 Narchuk/Shutterstock.com; p. 6 Natursports/Shutterstock.com; p. 7 Andrew Bret Wallis/Photographer's Choice RF/Getty Images; pp. 9, 22 Ian Scott/Shutterstock.com; p. 11 Durden Images/Shutterstock.com; p. 12 Patricia A. Jordon/ Peter Arnold/Getty Images; p. 13 Photo Sky/Shutterstock.com; p. 15 Wayne Lynch/All Canada Photos/ Getty Images; pp. 17, 23 Greg Amptman/Shutterstock.com; p. 18 Thomas Kokta/Botanica/Getty Images; p. 19 Jeff Rotman/Peter Arnold/Getty Images; p. 21 Reinhard Dirscheri/WaterFrame/Getty Images; p. 25 Alexander Safonov/Flickr/Getty Images; p. 26 Michael Aw/Lonely Planet Images/Getty Images; p. 27 Krzysztof Odziomek/Shutterstock.com; p. 29 (map) Peteri/Shutterstock.com; p. 29 (shark) Andrea Izzotti/ Shutterstock.com.

Printed in the United States of America

CPSIA compliance information: Batch #CW14GS: For further information contact Gareth Stevens, New York, New York at 1-800-542-2595.

Words in the glossary appear in **bold** type
the first time they are used in the text.

UNDERWATER THRILLS

Thrill seekers can find adventure all over our planet. Whether it's climbing tall mountains or jumping out of airplanes, there's plenty of danger around every corner.

Mountaintops can be breathtaking, but what dangers are hiding where you can't breathe at all? Which creatures are ready to eat anything they can find in the depths of the ocean? Sharks! From **massive** whale sharks to fearsome great whites, the oceans are populated with many kinds of sharks. Who would dare swim with hungry sharks? Only the bravest of thrill seekers! Read on to find out if you'd like to be one of them.

Predator vs. Predator

Polar bears are very large animals, but even they have been shark food. In 2008, part of a polar bear skull was found in the stomach of a Greenland shark. Scientists aren't sure whether the shark attacked the bear or found it already dead in the water.

Some people need excitement. And some people's idea of excitement is swimming with a predator like this!

More than 400 different kinds, or species, of sharks fill the oceans. Most sharks have several rows of teeth and powerful jaws. Many are meat eaters that chow down on fish, sea turtles, dolphins, seals, and sea lions. And they'll bite or even kill people who get too close. Sometimes people swimming in shallow waters at the beach are attacked.

However, some people actually *want* to share waters with sharks. With the use of special equipment and plenty of **caution**, it's possible to swim safely with these predators. Would you want to get close to one of these fierce fish?

Sharks have been in Earth's oceans for more than 300 million years.

Testing the Water

Most shark attacks on people are a result of mistaken identity. Sharks confuse people for prey and go in for the kill. Many take a "test bite." Most sharks swim away once they know what they've tasted isn't something they usually eat. There are about 100 shark attacks a year. Most aren't fatal.

DIVING IN

People at the beach may accidentally swim near sharks that like shallow water. But why would anyone *want* to get close to these fearsome creatures? Some people swim with sharks because they have to for their jobs. For example, **sponge** divers and even some kinds of fishermen may have to work in shark-filled waters.

Scientists studying plants and animals might encounter sharks looking for food in **reefs**. They also swim with sharks on purpose to better understand their life and habits. But some people dive with sharks simply because they think it's a fun activity!

First Known Attacks

One of the first accounts of shark attacks was recorded by ancient Roman writer Pliny the Elder. He wrote about a violent fish attacking divers in the Mediterranean Sea in his series of books *Natural History*, which was published about AD 77. Pliny the Elder called the sharks "dog fish" or "sea dogs."

Reefs are popular places for divers because many fish, including sharks, make them their homes.

THE GEAR

You often need special gear to be safe in the ocean, no matter what your activity. And if you want to go diving with sharks, it's really important to have the right equipment.

At the surface, a mask and **snorkel** let swimmers see underwater and still breathe. This is a good way to explore shallow waters. Many people wear wetsuits to keep their bodies warm and dry. Some wear flippers on their feet to help them swim faster. People may use different breathing tools for deeper waters, including oxygen tanks. Called **scuba** gear, this equipment is often the best way to dive with sharks.

Breathing Underwater

Divers need oxygen to stay safely underwater for a long time. On some kinds of shark dives, oxygen is provided to divers through tubes attached to tanks on board a boat. When divers need to go deeper, though, they have to carry oxygen tanks on their back.

This scuba diver holds a nurse shark!

Scuba diving in the ocean can be dangerous if you don't know what to do. Many diving businesses require divers to have special "open water" scuba training before they'll take them into the ocean with sharks. This means diving in lakes, seas, and oceans rather than in swimming pools where many people learn to scuba dive.

The Professional Association of Diving Instructors (PADI) offers the scuba training that many diving centers require before a dive in ocean waters. PADI instructors teach how to use scuba equipment and what to do if something goes wrong.

A PADI instructor works with a young student.

Dive sites such as those in the Neptune Islands of Australia require an open-water **license**, but South African sites don't require training at all!

Three-Step Training

PADI open-water training has three steps. First, you learn basic scuba information online, at home, or in a classroom. Next, you do a "confined dive" to practice basic scuba skills in a pool or similar setting. Finally, you do an open-water dive and begin to explore the ocean!

THE CAGE

To safely dive with sharks, you need a cage. Not for the sharks, though! People are lowered into the water inside a cage made of strong steel bars. The cage needs to be tough in case a shark decides to bite it or ram it with its body.

Dive cages are connected to a boat by cables. Cages are set to float at the surface or sunk to the seafloor. Some are round and just big enough for one person. Others are rectangular and hold several people. Many cages have viewing spaces so people can see well and take pictures.

Early Cages

In the mid-1970s, James Ellis invented the first shark-proof cage. The cage had a motor to help it move in the water. An opening let divers reach out and grab things. Ellis's invention was meant to help people diving for abalone, which are small snail-like creatures with ear-shaped shells.

These divers are getting close-up photos of a great white shark!

DARING DIVERS

Some people even dive with sharks without the protection of a cage! Commercial and film crews may not use cages to make sure they get clear photos and video of shark behavior, without cage bars in the way.

However, a few people think cage-free shark diving can be safe and more exciting if you know how to act in the water near the big creatures. One South African man even let his 5-year-old daughter go on a cage-free shark dive with him! Most divers don't **intentionally** put themselves around sharks without protection of some kind, though.

Chum Questions

People who dive with sharks spend money to see them, so sometimes shark-diving businesses chum the water. That means throwing a mixture of fish pieces into the water as bait. Chumming the water works well, but it means hungry sharks are looking for food. Many people think chumming makes sharks link people to food.

This camera crew doesn't bother with a cage as they try to get the perfect shots of tiger sharks.

17

GREAT WHITES

When people dive with sharks, they see many different species. One of the most fearsome is the great white. Growing up to 20 feet (6 m) long and weighing more than 5,000 pounds (2,270 kg), these white-bellied sharks can swim 15 miles (24 km) per hour.

Great white sharks are responsible for more than a third of all shark attacks on people. With up to 300 razor-sharp teeth, they mostly eat sea lions, seals, sea turtles, and small whales. The largest predatory fish on Earth, great whites can sense a single drop of blood in 25 gallons (95 l) of water!

Flying Sharks

When hunting animals swimming near the surface such as sea lions, great white sharks may first go deep underwater. Then they use their powerful tails to race to the surface as fast as they can, before the prey can swim away. Great whites may lift themselves completely out of the water!

BULLISH BRUTES

Bull sharks are some of the most **aggressive** sharks in the sea, and many knowledgeable people think they're the most dangerous. Bull sharks get their name from their **snouts**, which are short and wide like a bull's snout. Sometimes they head-butt their prey before biting down!

Bull sharks live in salty ocean water, but they can also survive in **brackish** or freshwater. Some bull sharks have been found thousands of miles up the Amazon River in South America. Bull sharks like shallow waters, which puts them near people swimming or surfing. They'll eat any fish they find and may take a bite out of a person because of this.

Breaking In

In 2013, a man named Bryan Plummer took video of a shark squeezing its head between the bars of a shark-diving cage off the coast of South Africa. The divers dove to the bottom of the cage to avoid the shark's jaws. The video was a big hit online!

Divers love seeing the aggressive bull shark in action.

STRIPED SHARKS

Tiger sharks are another shark divers look for. They're named for the stripes they have on their back when they're young. These sharks can live up to 50 years and are as aggressive as their namesake. Tiger sharks' jaws are strong enough to crack the shells of turtles and clams.

Scientists think tiger sharks don't have a great sense of taste, which leads them to eat all kinds of things, such as license plates. One was even found with a suit of armor in its stomach! That means tiger sharks don't always leave once they realize people aren't fish. That makes them very dangerous.

TIGER SHARK

Tiger sharks, great white sharks, and bull sharks are responsible for almost all shark attacks on people.

Sensing Electricity

Why do some sharks attack shark cages? Sharks have body parts known as ampullae (am-PUH-lee) of Lorenzini that can feel a weak **electric field** coming from the metal bars of cages. This causes sharks to attack. The ampullae of Lorenzini are also a way sharks find prey. All live prey have an electric field.

HAMMER TIME

A hammerhead's **unique** flat-shaped head makes it a popular diving attraction. Its eyes are very far apart, which allows it to see food easily. Hammerheads love to eat stingrays, animals that like to hide by burying themselves in sand. It's likely that hammerheads' ampullae of Lorenzini help them sense the electric field stingrays give off.

The great hammerhead is the largest of nine types of hammerheads. It grows up to 20 feet (6 m) long and weighs up to 1,000 pounds (454 kg). Hammerheads don't usually bite people, though some attacks have been reported. This makes them a safer shark to dive with, but people should still be very cautious!

Shark Proof?

South African inventor Norman Starkey invented a device to keep sharks away. Starkey's SharkPOD (Protective Oceanic Device) straps onto a diver's arm and leg and creates an electric field that kept sharks at a distance during several tests. However, when it was attached to a tuna, the sharks ate the tuna—SharkPOD and all.

24

In summer, large groups of hammerheads are often seen traveling north to cooler waters.

BIG FISH

Would you dive with the largest fish in the sea? Whale sharks can grow to be 40 feet (12 m) long and weigh an average of 20 tons (18 mt). These huge animals are bigger than a school bus, but they mostly eat tiny creatures called plankton. A whale shark has a flat head with a wide mouth that opens to filter water, letting plankton in and keeping larger things out.

People can swim near these gigantic fish in places like Australia, where they like to feast in the Ningaloo Reef. Whale sharks travel there between April and July each year.

WHALE SHARK

It's lucky for these divers that whale sharks aren't meat eaters!

Banned?

In 2012, shark cage diving was banned in Western Australia after four people died in shark attacks. Officials said studies showed that shark diving changed the behavior of area sharks. Southern Australia, including the popular Neptune Islands, continues to draw people with its shark-diving operations.

DO YOU DARE?

Swimming with sharks can be dangerous, but with the right training and equipment—and your parents' permission—you could dive right in! You can even swim with whale and nurse sharks at aquariums and amusement parks.

If you're looking for more thrills, you could vacation in South Africa or Australia and dive with professionals. You could also go to school to learn about ocean animals and get a job studying sharks all over the world. The more we learn about these animals, the safer we can make the waters for sharks and people alike!

Uncommon Danger

Intentionally putting yourself in the ocean near sharks is very dangerous, but deadly shark attacks are actually not very common for swimmers. Scientists say people have a 1 in 63 chance of dying from the flu, but just a 1 in 11 million chance of dying from a shark attack!

People are diving with sharks all over the world! Here are just a few shark-diving hot spots.

Shark-Diving Hot Spots

Farallon Islands, California

Point Judith, Rhode Island

Montauk, New York

Tiger Beach, Bahamas

Guadalupe, California

Mossel Bay, South Africa

False Bay, South Africa

Neptune Islands , Australia

GLOSSARY

aggressive: showing a readiness to attack

brackish: a mixture of salt water and freshwater

caution: care, thoughtfulness, and close attention to avoid risks

electric field: an area of force surrounding a body with electrical charge

intentionally: on purpose

license: proof that says you are allowed to do something

massive: very large

reef: a ridge of sand or a chain of rocks or coral at or near the water's surface

scuba: an acronym that stands for "self-contained underwater breathing apparatus"

snorkel: a tube used by swimmers to breathe underwater

snout: an animal's nose and mouth

sponge: an ocean animal with a skeleton that has lots of holes

unique: one of a kind

FOR MORE INFORMATION

BOOKS

Bodden, Valerie. *Sharks.* Mankato, MN: Creative Education, 2010.

O'Neill, Michael Patrick. *Shark Encounters.* Palm Beach Gardens, FL: Batfish Books, 2008.

Schreiber, Anne. *Sharks!* Washington, DC: National Geographic, 2008.

WEBSITES

Scuba Diver
padi.com/scuba/padi-courses/diver-level-courses/view-all-padi-courses/scuba-diver/default.aspx
Learn more about scuba diving certification.

Sharks
animals.nationalgeographic.com/animals/sharks/
Discover the world of sharks with cool games and facts.

Shark Week
dsc.discovery.com/tv-shows/shark-week
Watch videos and shows about sharks on this Discovery Channel site.

INDEX

ML

7-14